Taking Jesus off the Cross
from
Opus II
The Book of Earth

A rock opera

By
Steven Machat

The School of
Sacred Knowledge

The Colonization of Earth and the Making of Mankind, Taking Jesus off the Cross, The Book of Earth-Opus II, The Trident Copyright © 2021 by Steven Machat   All rights reserved. Printed in the United States of America and in the United Kingdom.

Except as permitted by the United States Copyright Act of 1976, no part of this publication may be reproduced, stored in a retrieval system or transmitted, in any form or by any means, electronic, mechanical, photocopying, recording, or otherwise without the prior written permission of the Author or the Publisher.

Cover Photo – Capuchin Monastery Catacombs

ISBN-13: 978-1-63795-985-5
ISBN-10: 1-63795-985-0

For more information on Steven Machat and The Book of Earth please visit www.stevenmachat.com and www.theschoolofsacredknowledge.com

God and me
God and we
Me and God
We and God
Are all
One

ACT TEN: Taking Jesus Off The Cross.

Jesus did not die on the cross let alone die for our future sins. Here is the true story of what happened as well as why it happened. How it was set up and what happened after Jesus got off the cross.

Metaphysical Awareness

This is the Act and its metaphysical vibrations that still runs our world of today. I will call this story the Crucifixion.

This is a deep state game. A deep state of Core people who set up the act a few hundred earth years before the curtain would rise and the masses can see or hear about the conclusion of the play.

This is so important for me to explain to all of us. It took me a lifetime to write. It took me a lifetime to understand. This series of acts is written to show you how I came to this conclusion.

I ask you all to open the portals of your third eye as you read or hear and reread and hear this act.

I write to share with all that we are more than just a physical body with a mind that tells our body what to do and when to do it. We are a consciousness locked in this body.

It's hard for you to believe what I share because we were not taught any metaphysical truths. None. But yet the few who rule over you were taught these truths on an as needed basis. The puppet masters, whose physical life spans far exceed mankind's physical existence use each new generation to perpetuate their existing global control of mankind's physical existence here on Earth. It is a dark cloud that shrouds our metaphysical conscious existence to make us stay in the matrix that this play The Crucifixion was created to destroy.

We are energy and our bodies that we live in are dense and are made to not let in the light of what we are as well as why we are.

Our energy, the energy of life, is from the beyond. Our energy responds to waves that come into our physical mind and shuts us down from operating outside our bodies and makes our energy operate inward. Meaning, living and allowing fears of uncertainty to make us eat our insides because we are fearful that things we want physically are not going our way.

We are all equal in consciousness. And we are not equal in our bodies. We can all do different things. We can do things that help all of us when we operate as a team. When we do things with the energies of fear and create an Us vs Them worldwide religions with imperial governments we have divided ourselves and live in a dark energy. The dark energy are the fallen angels that myths call Satan and Lucifer. Satan and Lucifer who use their magical powers of division and make you believe you are now living in their light which is nothing but the darkness, the veil over the one God. This veil, the puppet masters have you believe, is the "viel" which means greatness beyond all possible comparisons.

We are not taught metaphysical truths on purpose. The puppet masters have created an education system which prohibits you from believing anything that your physical senses cannot physically tell your mind exists. Your mind responds to only physical urges. My goal is to show you how you can override the fears and uncertainty your mind creates so you can live and experience a metaphysical love and joy not just a physical existence of serving the few who perpetuate the puppet masters' game.

WHY?

Because this evil system, the matrix of our imperial religions and governments would come crashing down. If you reverse the spell of the word evil you suddenly can live.

The Trident is three pronged. On the left if we are looking north is the energy we call left. It goes with our sun's movements around our universe. We are taught this is counterclockwise.

On the right side of our bodies looking north is the energy married to the energy of the earth. That energy we are taught goes clockwise, meaning dependable, predictable and therefore reliable. This clockwise energy we call conservative as it is the energy we in physical form wish everything to remain the same.

We call the right energy conservative and we call the left energy liberal. Liberal because they are able to feel that going round and round the same every day, something is wrong. Physical life is not predictable nor dependable as physical life must learn how to respond to the energies that come to Earth and change the vibrations of all living energies on Earth.

I must now share one naked truth and it's so important to see from the beyond what I'm sharing with you. Most of those who think they are turning left to make the world a better place in fact, join the right and become one of the new few who the puppet masters use to show the masses that if you behave and obey you can become one of us too. Understand that no one trying to change the system from within the system will ever change the system they will only become part of the system. Only by showing others that this new system will serve them better than the existing system will the chosen leader rebalance the lopsided energies that exist with this evil force that enslaves us and makes us believe that the two sides of a one-headed imperial government and imperial religion are different. They both work for the same evil dark forces.

Earth itself is run by the rules of Earth set up by Mother Earth and her womb both above and below the land to allow our consciousness to have a machine which gives us a ride as a consciousness in an earth body.

However, and this is paramount, both my body and Mother Earth wishing things to be the same are ruled by the sun's energies as well as the universe's energies and our galaxy's energies and the energies from beyond which are all part of the Father God of everything and more.

Please feel what you read or hear. It's important and when we understand what I am saying we collectively can succeed and live in the here and now and ascend as the game of life exists to be played. We need to go back to Father GOD. But while alive we can live with GOD.

Living with GOD is different than worshiping the gods that made our body machines and tricked our consciousness into coming to earth to live in a paradise for all when in fact our bodies were made deliberately dense so we could not feel our eternal energies but only live our dense physical realities.

The story I am about to share tells you the third way. The third way is living with God in our present form. The balance needed of energies that converge and make us live in fear and be ruled by the few who keep us in their system/matrix of control.

At the time of the Crucifixion we had a disorder of energies. It was lopsided to the right. We have the Sadducees who were priests and kings saying they exist to perpetuate the gods' wants and needs which I call Marduk energies. We have the Pharisees who also were the right as they too existed to perpetuate the gods' energies which I call Enlil. They lived by a book of rules which told people what to do and when to do it all saying this is what god wants us to do.

There was a third energy that came into play. This energy used the right and the left but the player was more than one. The players were the Core few who using supernatural energies played this game called the Crucifixion to show all alive and their heirs that followed that neither the Sadducees nor the Pharisees and their Roman rulers with their armies can determine the physical life or death of a rebel. A rebel energy comprising a team of Core beings is one to change the lopsided redundant ruling order.

But the rebel needs a team. One man alone cannot change the tides of locked up energy in the minds of mankind. There is a central figure but that central figure is part of a team. and the team will create an outer order and an inner order. The outer order goes clockwise and the inner order goes counter clockwise. The core, the team, is the energy required to make the opening of our bodies so the new way is accepted as the righteous way.

This act was to show you that no man made gods can act for the ONE GOD of all. And if we learn to use the energies from beyond subject to our bodies physical limitations the world is our oyster and is here for us to build our dreams. Dreams that must allow for all to participate when they wish to join and be more than just another brick in the wall. And if they like being the brick it is their right and we must take care of our living and the living must join in and participate in building the communities of mankind that live in the now not their grandparents' past world order.

Now let's go to Act Ten. This play still reverberates to this day which is misunderstood deliberately in our minds and shuts down our third eyes to the glory of the One God of all.

Scene One. The Metaphysical Truths of the Act of the Crucifixion.

Who are the Essenes? I spent most of my adult life researching this ever since I discovered working on the Last Temptation of Christ that something was up.

Notes on the Essenes. My research. The game was played from 500 BC to now.

The front vs the behind the scenes game.

The process of creating this movement begins.

How do we understand how we really are? We, being mankind. How we were created and why?

How do we stop worshiping wrong idols who call themselves gods?

How do we teach there is only one true Creator?

How do we teach that our bodies are not who we are?

Our bodies are Mother Earth creations with our consciousness from Father God locked inside this body.

The themes are simple and hard to endure.

Themes to teach the young ones. Lifelong purity. Avoidance of oaths or falsehoods.

All to direct you to see the truth. Recognizing a good providence alone shows their love of the Creator.

Love of virtue as opposed to the pursuit of money, worldly position and pleasure.

Love of mankind in their kindliness, their equity, their fellowship goes beyond the spoken word when a thought is confined by the written language rules of that age. Ever realize that rules of grammar limits you which is why lyrics and poetry says so much more?

One must ask what is physical life? Well it is the merging of spirit with the bodies of earth. How do you create life? Well it begins with one or many thoughts. An initial thought that becomes a virus. And this virus wants to make life around this thought. So the virus invades an existing structure and restructures it.

How? By taking control of the cell's brain called a nucleus. And then once in control creates the new outer existence which now exists to build its framework structure. This is the electron.

The inner controls keep the reason of birth going forward. This is called the Proton. However, please note, the Neutron in all life is the core of your life and the spiritual reason that this new life came to share. All living physical or imaginary organizations have the sun which I call the nucleus and the inner (Proton) and outer (Electron) thoughts circulating around the spoke of this life's new circle of existence. The outer goes clockwise and the inner goes counter clockwise while the Neutron is what they spin around.

Ok you now ask. Thanks for this metaphysical explanation on how life works. What is this connection with the Essenes and what was Jesus the man's role in this game you are about to share with us?

Well, here we go. Let's start with the Damascus Document. What is this?

These scholars of antiquity teach us that this is the entire works of the ancient Essene community of Hibirus called Hebrews and now referred to as Jews living in the community known as Qumran.

I must take a break from the narrative before I continue and tell you I will use the words of today to describe the players/actors of the events you are about to read. These names throughout mankind's written history were changed so you would not be able to put together the story you are about to read.

Let's begin with the words Jews, Hebrews and Hibirus. The Hibirus were so named by the god Enlil to let Abraham know that all Abraham's tribe males must be circumcised so Enlil can see who's on his side or on his nephew's Marduk's side.

Well that was back around 2200 BC. Enlil is called home to planet Nibiru. His Hibiru's have no living god leaders. They are waiting for their god to return. A lot goes on as Marduk now in control takes this tribe and uses them as chips you collect when his civilizations that he controls start killing each other for sport. Really a checker game.

So now without leadership from above, living here on earth the Hibiru's, whom I will call Jews, create a world of Laws which is Enlil's world order or authority which is Marduk's way. Pharisees vs Sadducees.

Enki did not disappear. Enki was just not there in the olden world of our Old Testament. With the Kaloos, as we learned in Act Seven and Act Eight, now I will share that Enki's energy created the third Hibiru order. The Essenes.

There are three versions of the Hibiru's sect. The Essenes are the third sect. The Essenes were a complicated sect. They had an outer grouping and an inner grouping. The two worlds were created deliberately. The outside world, their electron, you saw and the inside world, their proton, that only those who needed to know knew.

We are taught today these people were Jews. Something not right with that statement. Each change of the words creates a spell for you to see as you breathe in the meaning of what you are learning. The word Jew as opposed to Hebrew is one beginning as it removes your understanding of the supposedly common god. The word Hebrew as opposed to Hibiru makes you not see the origins of the word and where that word came from in the first place.

So I will now repeat, in other words what we just read, about Hibirus and Hebrews. The word Hibiru is what Enlil called Abraham and his followers' tribe. Abraham was the father of the Hibirus when he began as a stargazer known as a Chaldean. This initiation to becoming a select Hibiru from a god began when Abraham spoke with Enlil and said he would spy on the communities of mankind that were working for Marduk. Abraham's role was to report who was loyal to Enlil. So those male soldiers loyal to Enlil were required to cut the foreskin attached to their penis' off and now this ceremony made them Hibirus. Why? Enlil said doing this circumcision allows us to know you are Hibiru, just like us from Nibiru. Marduk's crew had foreskins. So now you know the difference.

Once done that male and his spouses whom he reproduces with will now belong to this Hibiru tribe that was to serve their one god Enlil and not any others.

Really important that you understand this difference so you can be released from the matrix you physically live in and judge others lives by and through. See the origins of the thoughts which control your emotions.

There was no J in any language at this time of earth's existence. Know that as this letter J was created to control all our thoughts about Jesus, the man originally known as Essu or Issu and the Hibiru's now called Jews.

It is how we build a matrix of controls. We give you symbols to make you act as well as react. See beyond the limitations of our minds. As we progress this section will open your minds to see the meaning of the play called the Crucifixion. The team that made it happen from beginning to end.

I will now proceed with the Crucifixion tale and latest attempt to change a world based on and of Sadducee or Pharisee rules of order. An order, that unfortunately, till this day, still controls our minds and makes us the dogs of the few who play the game creating fears and then removing the fears they created and in doing so we agree to allow their protons to rule over you. This is the game of our matrix we live in. The game is Imperial religions and their Imperial governments run by the secret core where property is protected not people.

As we learned in Act Eight new forms of understanding began to emerge around 500BC. Why? There was no Marduk or Enlil living on earth ruling the roost. Temples were empty. Churches did not exist. There were centers for healing.

Everyone was looking for their god. Their savior. Prophets appear and tell the story of the coming Messiah. The one with the message of the return of the gods. We were created to obey. When fear sets in we obey. But obey who and for whom?

The crucifixion tale was set up to open our minds to the beyond. To show us that God is everywhere and no one owns God. God loves all God's children. But you must also learn to love Mother Earth, your Mary. The womb that gives us life here on earth.

Now without further ado please sit back and learn the game played by the inner core of the Essenes and the game the people saw only on the outer shell of this game. The game was to show you that these two forms of government(Sadducees and Pharisees) did not speak for the GOD of all.

God of all loves everyone. God's love is not conditioned on any voodoo or religious ceremonies or clothing one must wear to be with God. For God lives inside us all. And if you wish to speak to God you do not need a third party to do your talking.

Jesus upset both ruling cliques of his era. He was sentenced to death for not following their ruling ways. The Crucifixion showed all that these two forms of government control did not speak for God when the body was not found.

All set up with intention to plant the seeds of Love which those who played the game believed would sprout and take over at a later time. They knew someone would put the pieces of the puzzle they left together to show all that God is not an object. God is love and love is God.

Now the curtain drops and the story is on center stage.

Scene One(i) The Essenes

Well according to our current historians these Hibiru Essenes fled to the desert areas in the Palestine region where they built the community of Qumran. The real diaspora then occurred during Antiochus IV Epiphanes (God Manifest) persecution of Palestinian Hibirus region which the Hibiru's called Jerusalem. This Essene group fled to Qumran.

This Seleucid King Epiphanes of the Hellenistic Syrian Kingdom, who encouraged the Greek culture of questioning orders as long as you accepted their ruling Syrian Kingdom order, is the one who brought on the war of the Maccabees a bit later in time. The leader of this army, King Antiochus III's son was captured by the Romans and served as the Romans hostage for his dad who was the ruler that the Romans allowed to stay as long as he obeyed their ruling order. Antiochus III's son was released when his dad died. As he was trained in the Roman way to see the world, his servitude had him adopt the Roman ways of controlling life to make his subjects obey the Roman way.

The exact time that the Damascus Document which outlines the outer world of the Essenes was written is not known but it was definitely before the supposed diaspora of the Hibiru labeled Jews by Roman Catholic Church his-story lines.

The Damascus Document consists of two major sections. The "exhortation" sets forth the sects outside for public consumption, living under the rules of Enlil order to exist. In fact, it made them very religiously orthodox to the outside world. This was what the inner sect, doing their work to change the world, were told to do. Hide behind this shield.

This section said that the outer order, the metaphysical protons, they were to live and emphasize their fidelity to the one god Enlil. They would strictly observe the sabbath, or special weekly day of prayers to Enlil and all other holiday days set forth to worship Enlil and those who passed worshiping Enlil at all costs.

Part two was the secret of this sect. Part two introduces the sect's enigmatic leader. The teacher of righteousness. It sets the stage to challenge the wicked priest of the East (Sadducees) as well as to challenge the laws and black and white order of the Pharisees.

This was the revolution to bring love into the equation of community rules and order. The love of the creator of all including the gods as the Nefilim called themselves. And their order where they required their servants and slaves known as mankind to worship them exclusively.

This second section also contains a list of rules, called today statutes dealing with vows and ritual purity, needed to enforce the thoughts that go against the matrix of life in their region. And they must be kept secret or else the opposite manifestations of thoughts will get them killed. Unfortunately naked truth.

It gave the members guidelines for community assemblies. Also the selection of the elders who should be judges for all, not for the few and their wicked lifestyles.

Last it contained the duties of those called Guardians that control admission to this Essene outer and inner sect and instructions of the new duties the new members must follow. This is the Trident of this system.

These documents and also the Dead Sea Scrolls are planted by the community leaders to be found. Their bet was someone would one day, when the time was ready, tell the tale of the game they played to end the sin of Marduk vs Enlil.

This is what the Kaloos of Enki's thoughts tried to share and help impose on others as the new way of mankind structures of rules with order.

The song by Donovan "The Hurdy Gurdy Man" may say it best.

Histories of ages past
Unenlightened shadows cast
Down through all eternity
The crying of humanity

This then when the Hurdy Gurdy Man
Comes singing songs of love.

It is time I believe. So let's continue on and hear the cries of eternal life and love.

Names given to you by your parents signified who you were and where you came from as the name represents what your parents thought at the time of your birth. So the Hibiru name Ezra means, in their time, salvation. Salvation to the Essenes was a continuous living need.

Ezra was the middle priest between the First Temple and the Second Temple of Jerusalem. He is also the man given credit for codifying the rules of order of the Pharisees. He is also the man required in the play of the Essenes. Ezra was the one that set the stage with proton rules, the outer rules, which must be observed to protect the Hibiru from further attempts by Marduk's legions in Babylon as well as elsewhere to destroy what remained of the Hibiru.

Marduk, we have learned in the Alexander Act, was dead. There was apparently no living Nefilim god on earth. Time to set the stage to meet the only God and so Ezra is important in this play.

Ezra did lead the Hibiru living in Babylon back from their exile to Jerusalem. And he created the Pharisee way of rules and order as a mandate to follow. This Essene game needed this orthodoxy.

Cyrus was a very important player. Cyrus, the ruler of Babylon, sent the imprisoned tribe of Enlil back home to Jerusalem. This move, Cyrus delivered. As he delivered the Hibiru their new lease on isolation from Marduk's Babylon. Cyrus let them go to their space that their ancestors dreamed about and called home.

They were home now with a mixture of Greek philosophy coupled with Zoroastrians thoughts married to the Torah and now called the Talmud.

Why was this a breakthrough? Because the absolute ruler (Sadducee) was about to be mixed with the rules of law and order. Order from a god and mixed with some philosophy. The Pharisee way. These two would mix and become our imperial religions of today with their imperial governments.

Still no communities of mankind living and sustaining life for all and all for one.

The Essenes tried in their scriptures to get you to follow the matrix of everything, not just the matrix of rules and order for the few who tempt you with scraps to make you live in their evil god ordered way.

But you need to understand the Essenes way was two fold.

One to exist in peace to the outside world by appearing ascetic, pious and really a pacifists' group who wanted peace before they would use their fist.

The second was to set the stage to have a central casted figure represent the visual image that God is love and love is God. This was a secret play being set up to get others to believe in the myths this human play would give society the vision to see God is from the beyond and loves us all.

Unfortunately, what this does is allows a song, vibrations of love, to become a visual image of control. Please hear my awakening as a thunder in your heart. Love has no face. Love is that simple. Love makes you smile, not beg or obey.

The cast of characters for this staged play were the apostles of the lead actor of this staged event. But they are not the same as the disciples. The disciples that history lets us learn about in the rewritten order have us follow the path that perpetuates the story that the imperial ruling order called Western society wants us to believe. Believe so their rules and order become our truth as opposed to the naked truth?

Scene Two. The Kaloos.

Let's review Kaloo.

This section will show you how the Kaloos deliberately set the stage using the Essenes and creating communities so that metaphysical energy could exist to make the play of surviving the crucifixion work. For the play to work the righteous one must survive alive after being nailed to the cross. In the time of the Essenes they were called the ancient ones. Or wise ones. They were from a very ancient race of mankind. One that lived longer than others as they were Enki's newest creations.

They were thought to come from the west. They stopped in Egypt and Greece first and opened the Schools of Sacred Knowledge that we know about still today. The Essenes called their home the Old Land in the West. Which may in fact describe Enki and his home Atlantis.

The Essenes, actually in their scriptures just like Plato, knew of the large land of Enki's paradise. It was an island with many surrounding islands just like England and Japan. Unfortunately these islands of Japan and Britain started with the Kaloos theories and ended up with Imperial armies of religious and government controls. North America started with equal communities living with nature too. It lasted until the imperial armies with their imperial Christ form of religions came and killed those then living there saying we, your conquerors, represent Christ. Our god. Their god of physical possession.

All these originals Schools of Sacred Knowledge had a very basic structure. There were the outer mysteries involving ceremonies all could take part in. The Inner Mysteries were accessible only by those trained in deep mind control to focus and open up their portal, their third eye, to energies from the beyond.. Focus to get to the transformative initiatory process required to understand so you could join your higher power once again in the beyond.

It's what the Masonic order that the Catholic Church tried to stop. However this masonic order did not have the knowledge of this book in their 33 degrees which the public knows but the core that created that masonic order knew about and lost.

This book series, Opus 1,2,and 3 looks at life as a continuous flow. We are just visitors living in Mother Earth's body in this time and space. There is a matrix that controls your thoughts and minds in place when you are born as we discuss. Then they only knew what was allowed to be read. And my truth is with the intent to help me find the answers I seek and my understanding of life in the first place, am I able to connect the worldwide dots in this age of Aquarius.

The earlier Sacred Schools did teach an energy system of the living so you could communicate and make shit happen that we call miracles. Using energy that if you do not understand how to use it you will never be able to recreate the things built with that sacred energy that was used.

The Kaloos told tales of their land sinking and this group took their ships and went to the land we call Egypt thousands of years before. Trying to make a new world order when the time was right to plant the seeds to be sown of LOVE. You will learn these truths in Opus 3.

By the time of the Essenes the craftsmanship of this being was reduced to just teachers and messengers of how to live eternal life in physical form. Remember we do not die our bodies do.

The Kaloo stored their sacred knowledge and it is said in scrolls as well as crystals. The crystals are stored somewhere here on earth waiting to be found. We only know of the scrolls. However you can read them when you learn to use your third eye portal and travel to your higher powers and get into the Ashki records.

I believe the role of the Kaloos was to get this info to the scattered ones. The ones who got out of the olden world of Anunnaki imperial rules and their wars by the two gods (Enlil and Marduk) of our Old Testament bible living in and with human form.

The whole inner game of the Essenes then and there in this region of the Dead Sea Scrolls was to prepare the energy that the Great Teacher would need to get the message of Love out and seen forever and evermore. It needed to have energy to keep the body alive. Super natural energy. More than just what is here on earth.

It was required by the Kaloo teachers that the Essene communities find remote areas so as not to draw attention to what they were about to do and why. Hence the desert. And the desert that was needed, needed a coast so people could travel to and from and not be observed by the many.

True support for this teacher required a system that would take care of the teacher. Nourish the teacher with love and protection. Feed the body and mind and inspire his higher consciousness to believe in what he was about to do.

The Essenes of Jesus were firmly entrenched but not just in Enlil's order. They were heavily engaged in Zoroastrian and Greek concepts of duality of life. The duality which the Chinese subscribed to in their mythology of yin and yang.

Again the communities of the Essenes were set up by the Kaloos. Everything so created as their communities were part of a triangle. Three posts called communities to keep the energy needed to pull this superfest of energy off, really a pyramid to attract the lights and contained that energy called electricity in this grid.

Their first community was by Alexandria, Egypt near the lake we call Mareotis. This was the mother household.

Then they set up Qumran. This house was the father's household.

Then they went on the path to Damascus. Why Damascus? Damascus was the center of the trading route from the east and west to the north and south. The cross of trade communications for each civilizations in those directions. Understand there was always a global worldwide trade.

Then these first three locations Alexandria, Qumran and Damascus each made three more sister communities as new triangles. New triangles to get their communities out and prepared to perpetuate the revolution of new thought called love.

At Qumran the new sites of triangle existence were Rama, Jenni and Mount Carmel. The one at this mount had only teachers, priests and students. No families which all the others had. This was the northern group. The southern group had its locations in Ein Gedi, Arad, Hebron.

All these villages understood the significance of running water. They were taught how to get it and use it. Water is an energy source. Maybe the most powerful earth based physical force of all.

Again these Essene centers were put together to use earth's energies to create the energy with a shield to pull off the play of Crucifixion and survival not death which everyone assumes is inevitable. Who could endure that pain is your thought. Well if you have the energy and the shield and you know it and use it, apparently the believer and his teammates creating the energy shield believe it and this belief using this sacred knowledge made it happen. They each kept each other engaged and believing this was their contribution to mankind. Also, the teammates had a built-in time limit of how long Jesus could be on the cross no matter how much energy was being thrown, sooner or later the body would expire or blow up.

As I have learned and now share with you, the Dead Sea region is full of minerals. Minerals needed to make the field necessary to transmit the energy from the Universe focus on the object inside their minds. It is also a region that, I have learned, made perfumes including opobalsamum, which is very similar to myrrh. Myrrh is used to heal wounds on bodies.

The teachings of the Essenes were based on sharing. Sharing, they believed, opens the portal to merging the Universe with your life here on earth. Doing this merges everything into God the creator of all. God who is the cosmos and more.

Only with love, unconditioned love, in your heart could this be achieved. You needed to believe there was a God of all over and above those who ruled over you with their manmade accepted version of god.

Shinto of Japan and the Chinese Yin and Yang of the duality of life tried to teach this truth. We are all one energy field living in our body forms. Unfortunately in those two lands the imperial governments of Marduk won their physical jailed minds in our current concept of life.

The Native American Indians lived in a society of federated tribes. They shared when they could, and protected when they had to. But saying these truths let's go back to the Era of Jesus.

Secrecy in the Essene order was required because the use of tools to make things appear or happen if in the wrong hands would lead to absolute chaos. Like the atomic bomb did by using the knowledge of how to release atomic power by splitting the atom.

I believe we are ready to live love, as the other way of life and order with control has proven not to work. We need to build a community that provides for itself, a self sustaining system without an elite class of bankers and their Federal Reserve Notes, masquerading as U.S. Dollars, in control. The bankers job is ministerial in truth. Monkeys can be trained to do it. And these bankers are really monkeys doing and believing what they do is the way it was made to be run and controlled.

We are controlled by the scarcity the puppet masters of our imperial governments, religions and their banks create. There is no scarcity. And learn this truth and watch the earthlings called mankind change.

The Kaloo's taught their communities they built up in Egypt, Greece, North America, Japan, England and this region of the Essenes many skills that we call magic. These skills are what the Crusaders discovered existed as they explored the cellars of the olden world Jerusalem shrines that were buried to take control of and for the new world order called the Vatican Church.

Remember before the Crusades of 1096 AD the Vatican in 1066 AD excommunicated the Eastern Christian Orthodox Church. This Church has a thought process based on the spirit of Jesus as opposed to the image of Jesus wrapped as Christ in his Vatican inspired robes. And I must add in 1066 the Vatican had their Vikings invade England using the name Norman to make England once and for all a Catholic Nation.

What was found we do not know. The Vatican had their copies of the books they burned in Alexandria. Something was found. And anyone that said they knew was summarily killed by the Vatican's rulers who got their right to rule by playing this Vatican game of checkers.

To this day we are still searching for the Arc of the Covenant. We the people think It was what Moses got from Enlil. It is really what the Kaloos taught mankind when it was time to civilize the masses.

Again I must reinforce as if this is a baseball swing to hit the ball, the game which you do not see is you are living in either Enlil's civilized rules of law and order from a make-believe god or obedience to or Marduk's authoritarian rule with the use of force. Enki and his troops called the Kaloos civilized with knowledge of the physical mixed with the invisible. The Kaloos taught the energies of Earth, solar energy and star energy. The energy of our universe. Enki himself understood the cosmos forces that created our Universe, our Sun and our Universe as well as the gravitational force of attraction of these energies called Earth.

The Kaloos taught consciousness as well as energy. The concentration for both groups deals with the magic of number, sound, heat, light and the color you see when you focus on the physical or the unseen vibrations. Focus in the region of our third eye. The third eye is where the vortex opens so you can perceive the energies when you understand the vibrations of all life.

The skills the Kaloos taught can be analyzed or perceived in a few different ways. The themes my research shows me are those subjects which will be taught in discussions at the School of Sacred Knowledge once the COVID 19 quarantines ends.

Scene Three. The Disciples and the Apostles. Both Seen and Hidden in Plain View. The Principal Players.

The disciples handed down to us by history rewritten matrix borders are the following in no particular order.

1. Andrew a fisherman.
2. Peter a fisherman.
3. James a fisherman
4. John a fisherman

These four were sons of Zebedee. Zebedee in Hebrew means endowed by god.

When two of Zebedee's sons were called to serve, sons John and James were mending their nets with their father. Andrew and Peter were fishing. These terms of fishing and mending the nets when receiving the call to serve in the play identified with Jesus as the play, not the team of Essenes, means they were searching in fishing for the answers. The net was what they used to get the truth caught so they could share it in the ocean of their evolving minds.

In the lands that were colonized by what we call Native Americans, those tribes had their vision quest. Not seas to go fishing but seas of air to catch the thoughts of their ancient spirits. These spirits would help guide the searching souls beyond our sun to learn the reasons we exist. Theirs was a net these tribes used to keep near where they slept which was called the dream catchers. So the few leaders could remember when awoken their answers called visions they received in their dreams.

The point is we are all looking for truths that physical life alone does not answer. We are more than this body. I believe the Native tribes of North America were re-educated by the Kaloo. The southern American tribes were created to serve and get the metals the Anunnaki wanted. North America escaped this onslaught for the most part. So when the ships left the shores of Atlantis with new races of mankind similar to the others but different in spirit awareness these societies created a federal society. Not a central controlled society. Each took care of their own community not combining the two in any Imperial one god one nation rule.

Back to the Essenes in Jesus time.

The Bible says that these two sons, John and James, were not just fisherman but also businessmen working in their community as merchants. Meaning they could co-exist with the Sadducees and Pharisees order of that day. Now known as Essenes to the public.

    5. Philip
    6. Nathaniel
    7. Thomas

These three are without jobs in the description of soldiers called disciples. However they were fishing when Jesus appeared after the death play called the Crucifixion. So let's say for right now they were Fishermen searching for their spiritual fish of knowledge.

To clear up all confusing thoughts in your head please note the word "Jew" identifies those living under Roman rule in Jerusalem which was in the area called Judea. A Jew became those who killed Jesus as opposed to the Hebrews which were a religion, not a governmental organization. That's why Jesus to this day is identified as a Hebrew as his religion as opposed to a Jew from Judea. Jesus was from Nazareth, that was the distinction.

    8. Mathew.

Mathew aka as Levi in Luke, it is said, was a tax collector for the Roman government. In this job he would be perfect for the role in securing the stage so the play could begin with the death of the man and his resurrection by God to show you God is in control. Not the god who is worshipped by the Sadducees and Pharisees who asked the Roman rulers to have Jesus the man be put to death for questioning their god. The Romans killed Jesus not the Jews, as opposed to Hebrews, under their lying story of what happened. This separation of Jew and Hebrew is important for the stories of the Catholic and Christian world that still identifies Jesus as a Hebrew. In fact Mary, the mom, was a Hebrew too in the stories, now being rewritten using the word Jew.

Mathew with this job had considerable wealth in that living community. Tax collectors kept a portion of what they collected. This currency would help Mathew fund the play in action. Our federal reserve here in the USA, a private banking system gets our taxes before the government and keeps their piece of our taxes to make the government do what? Ask yourself why do you pay taxes? More on that later.

9. James.

It is said James was Jesus's cousin. But I believe as do many others that James was his brother. Mary the mom had children. She was a representative of Mother Earth whose role was to create new earthlings for Mother Earth. But the Catholic lie requires Mary to be a virgin who did not have mankind sins make the physical body of Jesus. As Jesus was born in this world without sin. Jesus was god. Jesus needed the vessel called Mary to give him, god in this lie, physical form. Really telling you that god cannot give physical birth alone.

10. Simon

Simon was the zealot as written in his-story. A Canaanite as opposed to a Hibiru. A star gazer. Simon was zealous in politics and anarchy. A politician of his day. But a politician for the one God. Simon joined Jesus and swore allegiance to this play.

A zealot is a Warrior of Imperial Gods ready to fight the forces of darkness for the glory of the Imperial God. Unfortunately, one must use darkness to burn through the veil that hides the light. This energy had to be channeled to the team to win and survive. Not an individual quest but a team that works together to accomplish the common goal led by a quarterback with his behind the scenes coaches.

    11. Thaddaeus was described as another task man.

    12. Judas.

Today he is described as the treasure of this play and the band leader who performed the game. The New Testament describes him as a thief and embezzler as written in John 12:4-6. Judas is the one who identified Jesus to the Roman legion when they appeared at the last supper calling him Rabbi in their presence. The word Rabbi was the signal to the Romans that this was their criminal who needed to be arrested and tried and then executed in the Roman barbarian way.

This man Judas had the hardest role of the play. Someone had to turn Jesus in so they could put him on the Cross and continue this massacre death march. Judas was the one who had the role to allow others to see that the real God of mankind would not kill as the rulers made you believe.

Where is Paul? Definitely a big player in this play but not a Disciple. Paul was an Apostle. Paul who was known as Saul was a plant by the Core members of this group. The New Testament Bible does tell you about Paul the new Disciple who joined the play when he saw Jesus resurrected after death. Here is where the Catholic Church, to perpetuate a lie, call Paul a Disciple as opposed to an Apostle. If the Catholic Church story acknowledged Saul/Paul was an Apostle, meaning a major player in the creation of this game, the Catholic Church story of Christ takes on a different meaning. We read he was a Pharisee.

The group we today call Jew. This Jew named Saul at birth becomes Paul and the man who created the myth of Jesus for all to hear and say the rest of their living days.

The word then was Messiah which in Greek is Kristos. Roman language it becomes Christian. Not Christ the son of god and god himself. But the son of God. And as the man said we are all the sons and daughters of the one God, the creator of all living things.

But who was Paul really? Paul was one of the major characters of these Essenes plays to allow mankind to understand that no one thought system owns the creator of all. And this game that was supposed to give people the belief that they too could reach and live without others telling them they talk to the one God for you.

Another man living then who is an important part of this play and is not one of the twelve Disciples I mentioned above was the man called Joseph of Arimathea. Joseph was a very important Apostle. Maybe as important as Jesus.

Arimathea was the man who got Jesus' body after death according to all four canonical gospels, means approved by the Vatican as true for their followers to read and hear about. There was no historical location of Arimathea. So let's look at the metaphysical meaning using a word to hide in full view the meaning of Paul/Saul and Joseph Arimathea living then and there.

Metaphysical to do what? Show you the picture of truth you will see when you put the pieces together hiding in plain view. Saul was a tentmaker. What is this? A tent to live in and under this tent. The tent that Paul once Saul is said to now do for a living. Saul is manufacturing tents. Tent to do what?.

Metaphysical- it is a way of life after his conversion to believing in the play called the death of Jesus the man now our savior who died for our sins. What are those sins? For not believing that these fake gods were truth and not living in their world that they believe you were made to live.

Jesus' sin was that he spoke of Love. The Love of one and love of all. Not division but unification no matter how rich or poor. Regardless of color or gender. All for one and one for all.

Joseph of Arimathea was a rich man by the living standards of his day. He was a merchant who had ships under his control. And he would go to England and get the tin from the Cornwall area that Rome needed to keep their armies armed with the latest inventions to keep their Roman empire free of those inflicted with Germs of rampant disobedience to the Roman rule of trade and commerce.

The word germs is what Julius Caesar called those living in the forest of today's German language people. Which included the Franco tribe too.

Now the rules of order of the Essenes in the inner or second section, the hidden knowledge considered the Pharisees and Sadducees as living the wrong path. They were considered Sons of Darkness and the inner Essenes were considered Sons of Light. Notice no daughters. Why? Again a daughter is Mother Earth's representative. The woman is loyal to Earth first, not the god of control. The women will do what she is told to do to perpetuate their ability to reproduce. This is again the sacred meaning behind the removal of women from the imperial religions of god. Still true today.

The Pharisees game was to perpetuate the rabbinic stream of their form of Judaism. The Pharisee rules. These rules of required order which we call the Torah and their Talmud governed many aspects of both family and individual life. Ezra as we learned solidified this nonsense. It is highly structured and codified so only the few who could read would understand their game owning your mind saying this is what our god wants. Obedience so we stay in control of our community. Truth is this makes me cry that all die giving away their powers to this bullshit of voodoo ceremonies called organized religion. Put on your robes and do what you are told is god's way. Women sit alone and man prays to their father god in the sky.

The Pharisees stressed this fearful ethics over theology. That's why today's so-called Jews have no written understanding what's next. That is also why today's intellectual Jews jump to Buddhism's new cults to help them understand the cosmological plan of life.

The true Essenes Brotherhood had a foundation. That foundation has the following principles.

1. Your Father is the Cosmos.
2. Your mother is nature meaning earth
3. Your brothers, and I must add sisters too, are your fellow mankind.
4. Live in harmony with those laws and forces of the Universe (solar energy) and nature (Mother Earth) and your own being.

All taught by the Kaloos on behalf of mankind's physical designer Enki.

Scene Four. Setting Up The Metaphysical Stage.

Let's now look at how this Crucifixion saga was set up.

As we read above the Kaloos studied the energy of earth, star and solar vibrations. They studied their charts to see what energies would exist on a given day in the future as well as what energy you have from your earth creation in physical form. They knew where the energy would come from on earth's time and land here in our gravitational bubble which includes our atmosphere. Apparently the Mayan, Aztec and Egyptian cultures were taught these energies and they were found in their calendars inside the temples of those earlier societies.

Tasks were given to the members in the community in line with the thoughts associated with your consciousness landing here on earth which we call birth, tasks for physical as well as mental and spiritual. The astrological birth signs we all pay to have others tell us what our life means.

The Essenes were taught this knowledge. And they believed in reincarnation to reunite with your past energies and therefore finish your purpose. If you like, take a moment and research the Islamic sect called Alawites who still believe in reincarnation. However, they do not discuss ascending out of this dimension of darkness to the eternal light of the One God of all. We as a consciousness all come for destiny and we agreed to be here in this dimension set up to teach lessons of some sort in the first place.

This particular play is to show you that the rules and order we the people are now submitting to are based on fears. There is no love in fears. You think god does not love you so you give away what our Creator gave us to be by following the current pied piper song to live other's destiny and that is your fate. You did not know God the one. This play was to show you who was the boss. Not those you worship. God was the loving father and you are the boss of what you do and why you do it. It is called free will.

However Mother Earth is the exclusive boss of our bodies. Time to learn this truth.

We have learned who the Disciples and Apostles living then were but we were never taught the game being played. As this game required a team to make it work.

The Essenes had their rules of secrecy. No one knew everything except the play creators. But the pieces of this play were scattered around our globe so the pieces could be put together at the right moment to show you what's going on. A Marvin Gaye tune I now hear in my head.

Jesus became the sun of this play, the spoke on this wheel of energy. The inner order was the wheel and the rest where the energy that made this wheel go round and round with the hope for mankind's eternity.

As it says in a Essene community rule which was found and translated into English from what we call the Dead Sea Scrolls in English: " All the children of righteousness are ruled by the Prince of Light and walk in the ways of light….And as for the visitation of all who walk in this spirit, it shall be …eternal joy in life without end, a crown of glory and a garment of majesty in unending light.

Power and a full picture of eternal love with the One. Not Jesus the man, but the Creator of All. Which Jesus was chosen because of his cosmic energy to lead the way in this play to have us all see and understand by learning the parts of the play which required teamwork and everyone working for all and all for the One.

Now in the Essene world, and this is what secret societies try to duplicate with their levels of knowledge, the Essenes had a world of three orbits. The outer ring of their matrix system was the Town Brothers. Their level of awareness of the game being played was limited and therefore they could speak what they knew as they knew only what they were allowed to know. These Town Brothers were loyal to the most visible ring of the theme. The outer order itself.

The next ring was those who lived inside the communities. They too were loyal to the Essene order. But here they saw a little more of what was being created.

Then there was the Core Group. The actors and directors and set designers and music-vibration of sound players. This group knew the game being played. They lived it and played it. They were removed from the Town Brother's sight. They were secretive and did not engage with the communities when they held their secret meetings.

The problem with this deception play is it is impossible to see and understand the picture of thoughts the game wishes you to learn and discover from any written records. You need to see the whole picture. And it will take a lifetime of questioning everything you hear to discover Love the way this play wanted you to understand and hopefully live.

I believe this is the spirit of Enki's last gift to us earth body creatures that he created in physical form. Enki wanted no part of his brother Enlil's orders and control of obedience as that is not love. Nor his son Marduk whom he did allow the Elders of the Nefilim to nuke Marduk's surroundings as we learned in the days of Sodom and Gomorrah. Unfortunately Marduk survived the onslaught and the elders of the Nefilim believed it was Marduk and earth's fate to rule earth till earthlings figured out this imperial order of control was the pure evil way.

So how those winds created by dropping their bomb on society did not get Marduk held up in Babylon was a puzzle to them.

The elders of Nibiru decided that the energies of that control earth wanted the lesson to teach what a mad man does when he gains power that he is not capable of living let alone leading others to the eternal life of LOVE.

This is the reason for the Essenes. To stop evil from ruling this planet so we mankind will not continue to serve the make believe god in the sky who says these rules were made by me for you to follow or else.

Scene Five. The Core Players Both Seen and Hidden in Plain View

The Core Members.

Who were the Core group members of this play? From the fragments of info that I can gather I will share what I know.

There was Joseph and his sister Mary. There was Mary's husband Joseph that had a son named James in addition to Jesus who also was part of this core. There was Mary Magdalene and John. After the death of Mary's husband Joseph this slot was filled by Thomas who later became one of the disciples of Jesus. Again remember there is no J in Hebrew or Latin nor Greek so I am only using the names we know in our 21st century matrix.

So we have six. Then there was a seventh whom they were waiting to grow into the position of control and the light that would give their wheel the energy to spin and create this living tale. This is the inner person and it was not Jesus. No Jesus was the central lead character. This man was Saul who became Paul. I will carry on so you see this game.

Notice how there is no Peter. Peter was the leader of the conventional outside characters of this play, a Town Brother.

He probably was not an Essene. To do what he did, Peter was better off not knowing the inner game. Peter became the people's leader of the Western Church of the Kristos message. The Messiah.

The Messiah. The central figure of this play. Jesus.

Well it is said by those who knew Jesus that this man was very balanced. Had a softness about him. Was gentle with the women and children. He was stern with men when he needed to be in debate for the common good of all. Jesus, it is said, had the ability to look right through you and see the vibrations of your energy to understand what your game was. And please note we all are players of the game.

Jesus has the energy that few have in a very balanced system that married no one thought of control. Jesus knew that thoughts become see-saws and must be neutralized to maintain a balance where it is not my side vs yours. It is both sides of yin and yang learning to balance and accept that everything has duality. And to live with eternity we must balance the physical wants and needs we call duality.

This was the Chinese theme of government. We have read about that. And yes I believe that Confucius was trained by the Kaloos.

What's my game? Get this out like I was told to do when I came here to earth. I am still the same with more wear and tear than I was. I play life and all I could do to get here and understand the weaknesses we have that makes us mankind with animal instincts laced with understanding from the angels and God the one Creator of all.

I lived life by following the waves that gave me the opportunity to travel and discover there is so much more than material possessions we worship over Love. We are raised to love objects. We were not taught how to share love and create love with fellow subjects. We are not the objects we own but our society of controlled thoughts says we are.

And yes I like possessing but never gave my life to live such an incomplete way. If I did I would be back again to learn lessons I was supposed to learn before. I feel I am ready to move on finally.

Jesus, it is said, had the unique ability to help all those he came into contact with to see the bigger picture. A picture that is so simple to see. We make the layers that make us believe it's complex and so hard to understand. We become confused and are led astray by our fears and wants and needs. Darkness surrounds our lives when we all believe we live in light. But that light is contained with the shadows of our fears that do not allow us to see the whole picture of existence. The God in all not just me or our team of the few not realizing this team is part of the all.

It is so important to run a balanced society to have a leader who is an elder. Not a merchant or a member of a thought that excludes all others. But an elder that sees the light in all thoughts and the darkness that will come if you follow that one stream or ray of light. You become blinded by your own light.

Scene Six. The Crucifixion

Now to the Play. The Crucifixion.

The game which I call a play is simple. Expose the lies of the current system you lived in and under. One that judges you for what you did not understand is that love is the order that does not need any rulers or rules for harmonic order.

We must learn from our past and live in the present. However we are trained to be judged for being one that is part of the established controlling order. You are not here to enlighten let alone for disagreeing with thoughts that control your mind and make you a widget in this system for the few that you let rule over you.

The imperial system in the imperial community controlled at this time by this play proved to be a lie. The core members and their unseen teachers decided to end the system by intellectually blowing it up. They blew it up with the creation of salvation and God's love as the take home message of this play. Unfortunately they did not realize how dense the masses were and they needed to worship the image of a god instead of living with God and by worshipping the image perpetuating the imperial religions and imperial governments. That dark energy took Jesus of Love and made him the Christ of control.

Love is the light that we should have and share with each other. We go through life living the seasons of our own personal existence learning to adjust and balance our wants and needs with the realities of our physical limitations. Making a final judgement of someone's past by a system of rules and order is a way to commit them to hell for ever more is wrong. Sentenced for what they have done as opposed to what they are now and will become when the light of GOD shines through their heart. To live in a society that tells you they have God's authority to kill you for what and who you are is a lie. You are then listening and following the devil.

So the play crib sheets are the following:

Jesus was the public figure to go forward and act out in full public view the climax of the Essenes mystery school teachings. The Essene community will then disappear after they clean up their existence in their today and our yesterday.

Jesus, the lead actor, will have five scenes in this play called the Crucifixion. 1) Jesus will be arrested. 2) Jesus will stand and go through a mock trial. One that is predetermined. Not one to hear and give a fair trial. No, it's a fixed decision. 3) He will be given the sentence of crucifixion. 4) He will take the walk carrying the cross in full view. 5) He will be crucified.

However now the unseen team will concentrate and send the energies universal and solar as well as earth energies needed for Jesus to play and survive the role he has to do in all his five acts listed above.

The energies that they were taught to create and project to sustain the game they are all about to play. Death by the system with physical rebirth from the cosmos energies we call God.

Now the energy which is generated and directed at Jesus will be both created by the player's meditations as directed by the Kaloo elders and the crystals the Kaloo taught them to use. The crystals were used to create the system needed to hold the energy created by thought and directed by the triangle of the three communities set up specifically to make this a complete energy system (the grid).

The Energy System.

You need to be open to understand or at least explore what I am about to share with you. This is metaphysical truths of energy. We are all energy. We are substances in the body that we see and can touch, yes. But know or try to learn that we are all particles too. Particles that vibrate and are in tune with the energies we come into contact with. This is explained in the two words theme "Quantum Physics".

So let's call the physical the outer energy of density. The moving vibrational particles that make up what we believe to be the body is the inner energy contained in our box. The box we call a body.

The Triangle did the following to keep Jesus alive on the cross. The outer energy, earth's energy focused and intensified by the crystals, was directed along the lines of force running across the surface of the land towards Jesus on the cross. This energy was needed for Jesus to maintain the living physical energies one needs to stay in the body physically alive bleeding on the cross.

The inner energy was fed by the communities into subtle levels for being directed to Jesus to feel. This helped maintain the desire to use the levels of energy to keep Jesus alive and in his body.

The central triangle was formed by energies from Jerusalem the main focus of this play. The Cave and Qumran being the other two locations.

The Cave was located in a hilly area to the north of Jerusalem. This was a location selected to make it equal with the other two somewhere between Jericho and Silwad. The total field is 120 miles if we measure it. This is what we call the ley lines that physical scientists and their science poo poo.

Now one can start to see the metaphysical meaning of a pyramid and energies that the pyramid can move as opposed to create on its own.

This energy system to create takes earth's time to do. That is why the society was so secret in reality. Only show the world what you want them to know. The game was to be orthodox Hibirus who just appeared to daven all day and night. While the community exists to feed those in their meditation all prayers.

Serving God whom the others believe is Enlil, the Hibiru god, long gone and to this day not forgotten. But notice how he never appears to save the Jewish day.

The Kaloo started this energy field, I have read in books, with fragmented information on the Essenes maybe 200 years before the play was ready to be staged. Their need was to have the energy field in place as the time got near when the righteous one would appear and take the lead in this game to show others what the one God really is. The One God is an energy force. We are energies from the One God living in the physical bodies so created by the Nefilim using the dust of earth modified with their extra genes they gave us earthlings so we could perform their circus tricks and serve them as slaves and servants. The Crucifixion was the intellectual play to make others see the game we are playing

Yes Jesus did die for our sins of allowing others to take away our life and make us obey their devil dark ways. Their way of control.

This system was based on the natural energy lines that run on the surface of earth. And the crystals just strengthen with its additional energy to make this triangle a truer geometrical form of locked up energy.

Now back to the living in their days of Atlantis. Those there had specialists who knew how to use crystals to box up energy in certain geometrical forms to make life persist and stay to exist in that certain geographic space.

So you can visualize this triangle please see the following. The first crystal is in Qumran the second is the cave. The third is Jesus the man giving his body up to the energy received by this crystal he has become to keep him alive as the game is played out.

Again please see this in your mind. The energy kept him inside his body. He did not leave when the physical pain was pain that he could not live in any awareness of being alive. He went to sleep but stayed alive inside his body.

Jesus and the Crucifixion

Jesus was a teacher
Ordained from God above
He preached that all humanity
Must learn to live in love

He told of one creator
Who would let us live in light
That all those idol worshippers
Could not have had it right

To make him pay for his beliefs
They put him on the cross
The Romans thought by killing him
Their rules they could enforce

But the Essenes had a different plan
So together they would scheme
To make his body disappear
As if in a mystic dream

So now this cast of characters
Set up this brilliant play
To bring to its fruition
Of whisking Jesus away

Joseph of Arimathea
Got Jesus on a ship
To a land then known as Avalon
Out of his killers' grip

By Debbie Veltri

Scene Seven. Taking Jesus Off The Cross.

Now let's go to the finish line of the game.

Joseph gets the body when Jesus is cut down. According to the accounts this was set up in advance by Joseph who was Jesus's uncle and the brother to Jesus mother, Mary. And Joseph as we learned was involved in the Roman world of trade. Big time. And I must repeat Joseph had the ships that went to Southern England to get the tin that was needed by the Romans to make bronze that was used to make the weapons to enforce Roman rules of order.

What does Joseph do with the body?

According to the Akashic Records which are in the air of our dimension and with the use of crystals those in the know can gather in their minds in physical form to review this story.

When Jesus was taken down from the cross the core group who were meditating in the chambers they called the "clear seeing chamber" dispersed. They knew that the authorities and military arm of the Sadducee was going to figure out the ruse.

The core went to the other building and told the group that the work with the energies went well. Jesus was out of the physical body but still in the body on a much lower level. He will now be revived.

The writings I have read say that Archangel Michael saved the day and kept him alive. This angel sign is the fire of life when you need his help to carry on. Those meditating got the energy of Michael to come and keep that physical life flame alive inside the cells that make protons go one way and our electrons of each cell circle the opposite way. Truth this is the sign we call Nazi. In the middle is the neutrons that when we are alive stores each cell the energy to stay in rotation. Lose that energy in your neutrons and all life as we know it ends. Then the cell without this super nature energy acts its part and disintegrates back to dust and we go back to the ethers to ascend or reincarnate.

Truths which many will argue can not be undone. Jesus the man and Jesus the spirit came to teach that eternal life was in our hearts and that energy never dies. That energy is the Cosmos. All part of the evermore Kingdom of God.

It is said in the Akashic records by those who can read the thoughts in these crystals of time that two died trying to keep focus on the crystal that was Jesus' heart in this game being played. It is very hard to throw energy.

Remember the story of the Crucifixion is a team game. Jesus was the lead actor and one who had the psyche ability to withstand the pain to teach us all that the real God, not mankind's religions of god is so much more than the Sadducees ruler or giver of Pharisees ruling order. God was everything and more. Just believe and you will see in the here and now the wonders of all life that God created with love. Not created for you to serve him as a slave or servant to the few who said god choose me over you.

Scene now changes to the tomb where Jesus is laid to begin his eternal earth nap. The next game which is hidden in plain view.

The tomb that now held Jesus was not a tomb. No it was a healing chamber. There was the outside entrance that was now covered with a stone. However there was a secret passage to get one inside the tomb without others seeing what was going on.

A tunnel was built by some of the Essenes that others did not know about. The tunnel began at Joseph's house. The entrance from the tunnel was a door on the inside that was wood. However if you were inside the tomb you would just think that door was rock, indistinguishable from the other rocks.

These people knew what they were doing. Everyone reported to the beehive which we will learn was Joseph and his sister Mary, Jesus uncle and mom respectively.

The healers, we are told, were Luke and Jesus's sister Clare. They were the Essene healers of their day. The most powerful who trained to nurse a spirit back into the cells so the cells would move to more than just stay alive. The spirit of God, the one that is called the Holy Ghost meaning in physical form one can not see it but it's real. We all have this energy or we would not be physically alive in body form.

The stone shut off outside light and shielded those standing outside from seeing or hearing what was going on inside the tunnel. The healers had their ointments and crystals to heal the body.

As Jesus the consciousness fully re-enters the body pain is the sound one heard. Unable to walk as he awoke he was carried off in a simple stretcher of that time. Into the home of Joseph they went.

The ruse was necessary as the Pharisees would go crazy to find the missing body which others were to believe rejoined the God of all. In spite of the rulers of this land the Sadducees and Pharisees with their Roman legions believed that Jesus, in essence the terrorist to their ruling regime, was dead, there was a big problem. Their rules and order made no allowance for a body just disappearing into thin air. So they knew something was up.

Joseph and the others knew that this tomb would eventually be inspected. So after they moved away the stone at the entrance to the tomb during the second night, now visibly empty, on the beginning of the third day, the community learned that the body was gone. Then the next day the stone was rolled back over the entrance.

Joseph quickly moved a new dead Essene from Qumran into the tomb before the authorities could get inside to figure out the game work that was done. This move gave the crew time to finish the escape.

The tunnel exit was on Joseph's land. A stable was built over the entrance to the tunnel. This stable was the cover they needed to put dirt inside the secret tunnel to hide what was beyond physical view.

The Pharisees wanted inside the tomb. The Sanhedrin (the Judges) were now in charge and the Essenes led by Joseph cried outrage. The cries of desperation were heard. You cannot invade the sacred space where the dead lie awaiting their religious burial.

Now the Sanhedrin would meet to decide what to do. Why? They were the judges or elders of society who decided what was right or wrong religious behavior.

The problem now was Joseph showed his colors and was to all those of critical thinking apparently the leader of this game. He had the money and the connections to pull it off in plain view. Joseph was the best supporting actor. Mary the mother was the best female actor and Mary Magdalene was the best supporting female actress in this game of showing that the Real God is not what you are forced by rules and order to worship and believe.

Jesus, because of this delay and the predetermined focus on a spot where he once laid, was able to get to Qumran and north to Damascus to find Saul the fake Pharisee. Now Saul becomes Paul. As Paul, he now tells all that he met Jesus the person who now becomes spirit in Paul's cover-up so as not to disclose where Jesus physically went. The physical Jesus asked Paul to be the messenger to let all know that he is alive and well. He did not want Saul to let anyone know where he was going so Saul/Paul, to protect Jesus's physical existence and to cover his own ass, told everyone that he saw the 'Spirit' of Jesus and his return to Father God. Paul would now spread the gospel which we call Gnostics of the new world order. The new world order is the Kingdom of Heaven governed by the God of All right here right now and to experience this Kingdom of Heaven on earth you must live a righteous life.

By Paul saying he saw the Spirit or the change of the narrative this becomes the story of Jesus ascending to god as for the first time a body could not be found and these primitive minds were unable to understand how the body could just disappear. So the story they were told was that Jesus' body disintegrated and that is why a body could not be found. They believed that the Holy Ghost took him from Earth back to father god.

There was no resurrection and that is why the religious Sadduccees and Pharisees knew something was up and their control over people's minds would now be questioned as they had no answer to where the body went. The people would now see that no king, priest or army could explain the absence of the body.

There is a big problem with the play as nowhere is it said which god Jesus rejoined. Nowhere did the playmakers account for the fact that Marduk's energy would take the lesson Jesus taught of the love of God was more powerful than the man-made gods that the people worshiped and turned the Love that

Jesus shared into a Christ of absolute control. This story is in Act Eleven.

Jesus taught love is God and God is love but because there was not universal figurehead to tell the story and the playmakers did not want Jesus to reappear to tell the story we have lived 2000 years traveling through the age of Pisces to the age of Aquarius where now the dots which appear all over can be connected to show you that the love of God is stronger than any King or religious order.

This game, played is very simple to feel. The crucifixion was staged and played so mankind could see once and forever more that no religion or government speaks for God and has the authority from God to say when one could live or when one must die.

Scene Eight. The Escape; Born to Run

Jesus.

So what happened to Jesus the living man? Jesus, after Damascus went to join Mary Magdalene in the Avalon region we call Glastonbury. I will soon share that story.

Peter who was involved was not mentally ready to believe in the eternal spirit. Peter became the one who spoke of the lies that the Nefilim taught. According to Peter, Jesus went to live in eternal form with god, his father. Jesus, the only son of god, was killed for our sins by the few who tricked the Romans to kill him.

The real sin was hidden in plain view. Our sins were believing those in charge of physical life masquerading as god's reps in fact threw God of all out. Believe in Jesus and you will be saved when you leave this physical world.

That is not what Jesus and this play was about. God the one is here, there and everywhere. Live the righteous life and believe in eternal love and you can in the here and now join God's realm of eternal life while being in physical form.

This is something the Buddhist's did not try to teach. Their teachers did not tell you how to get there now. The Essenes taught you how to run straight up the hill. The Buddhist taught you how to go round and round the hill each lifetime getting one small step closer.

It is so hard to believe when you believe in property as the reason you live. Property is an ornament to be worn or lived on. It is not to sell your soul and eternal essences of being here on earth. You will never ascend to the next living level if you are married to mammon (physical possessions).

Joseph plants the rumor that Jesus went home to God of all by turning to dust. This is what he planted in the minds of those living then. And this is what the Pharisees knew was bullshit.

The play went perfect. It caused the ripple it intended of man's ruling order in this region of Sadducee, Pharisee and Roman controls over the minds and physical bodies at that time.

The problem, as I said above, is there was no written decree of what the play meant. There was no visible leader of the team that spoke of this game. Now stories would evolve for others to try and take control of the game they were not prepared to play. The Sadducees and Pharisees had no explanation to calm the inquiring minds or their community. There was now a third sect of Hebrews and this sect said God is Love and Love is God.

The sect was given the name Christians by the Roman rulers, which in Greek means Kristos and in Hebrew means Messiah.

This sect was created to follow their Messiah, their Kristos, the man who showed them the way to the eternal God of all. The man who built a foundation for people's minds to understand that all mankind are equal and should live in a community based on community support not based on living to serve the few who you allow to rule over you. Building a world based on spiritual love without the need for orders to control. A true utopia, where everyone serves each other and where all could live their dreams in this land called Earth.

The problem of the matrix we live in this life in physical form is we need a boss. We need a father figure to fix things and assume the mother figure will always be there to love us when we need it.

Let's look now at Joseph the uncle, Mary, the mom and Mary Magdalene.

Let's call out the instigator as the revolution is here.

Who was Joseph?

Let's look to the gospel of Mathew. In these passages you can read he was a rich man. In Matthew we also can read it was he who obtained Jesus's body from Pontius Pilate. When he gets the body he wraps it in a clean linen cloth. With this wrapping Joseph takes the body to the tomb Joseph built out of rock.

Follow me. The game was already laid out. Pilate who was in charge of the hill we today call Golgotha which in Aramaic means skull was on alert to give the body to Joseph. By the way in Latin this was the hill of Calvary. The latin word which is created from the Latin word Calva bald head or skull. The hill of the dead.

In the Gospel of Matthew / Mark and Luke, Joseph is referred to as the counselor. In the Gospel of John, Joseph and John were mentioned as Disciples, but secretly in fear of the Sadducees or Pharisees, then lumped together as just John and called a Jew. A Roman word then to describe those who lived in Judea and were revolting against the Roman ruling order.

Joseph was Mary's older brother and therefore Jesus's uncle. When Jesus's dad John died, Joseph took over the masculine role of molding his nephew with Jesus's mother, Joseph's sister Mary.

The source of Joseph's power was his wealth. But not idle wealth. His wealth was his living and trade empire that stretches from Cornwall England and his tin mines to Jerusalem and everywhere in between.

Joseph controlled, like Amazon today, the US shipping trade. Joseph would deliver the tin to the Roman garrisons in need of that material. The material beginning as tin now smelted (alchemized) into ingots. He had a merchant fleet to bring the raw materials to be manufactured and then to the consumer. His fleet may have been the biggest then of them all. And know these fleets had soldiers who would kill to protect the goods.

And to play the game because of his wealth and family position he was a member of the highest social order of judges of the Hibiru faith called Sanhedrin. Plus he was a legislative member of the provincial Roman Senate. Joseph had power. The unseen power. That is until his game of being part of the inner core of the Essenes became outer truth.

Truths had to be hidden and Joseph was a master of hiding truths. Joseph did not correct people who took his parables the wrong way. Very few people then and to this day understand the metaphysical truths that they live in. This play without a teacher sitting there explaining how they kept Jesus alive on the cross is impossible for people to understand. People need a guide.

As many have said, truth is so precious at times it must be wrapped in lies. We can read in the book called the Drama of the Lost Disciples how Joseph. Mary and Mary Magdalene plus a few others were put into the Mediterranean Sea in an open ship without oars or a rudder and no sails. It was a ship that had nowhere to go and no true way to be to be navigated except by the winds and the currents of the air and oceans. In essence a death sentence.

This rumor was started by the Romans as they were paid to say on Joseph's behalf. The Romans needed Joseph's ingots and were only too happy to oblige. Now what's interesting is if you have the time you can look up Cardinal Baronius, a so-called leading expert of the Romans Catholic Church in the late 1500's AD. This Cardinal claims the current took the few to the southern coast of France. And hence the tales of the search for the Holy Grail of Wisdom that Jesus taught hidden in made up stories to get you not to see the truth.

Joseph had the ships and they all got out of their Dodge before the sheriffs of rules and order appeared. Joseph sailed to his mother's home land in south west England. The land we know from myths called King Arthur and his Avalon. His court of twelve. Get the connections. Always wondered the magic unseen of that number 12.

I spent many years of my life learning the folk stories of England. Knew there was more here. Was fascinated and throughout my life and learning the entire picture I saw the story unfold as if I was part of it back then. I get the ruse. I actually love the visualization of the fakes called Pharisees and Sadducees trying to figure out what went on. Where are the Essenes? All now long gone. They closed up shop. And understand that the third way were those who lived and believed in the message the Kingdom of Earth with righteous behavior by the community could be here and now and not next life. And this was so hard for people to believe that there was living energy that those who knew how to use it could make magic appear for those not trained to see the metaphysical truths of existence.

Where is Joseph's family home in England and why England in the first place?

Joseph gets mixed up as James, Jesus' brother in some of the tales of this story. Regardless, in Glastonbury one can see the resemblance of the sanctuary that existed in Jesus' time which became the Glastonbury Abbey for healing and learning the spiritual way. We are told it was a church which it was not.

Jesus and the others did not believe in a designated place to meet God, maybe the fake god but not God. God was within. There was no need for a temple nor a church to pray to anyone but the imaginary idol others created so you could withstand the pains that were inflicted by you in living in this unnatural manmade order by the few to rule over you.

The Nefilim were physically gone but their energies kept a veil on Earth and mankind still in this new dimension unsure why they were here, lived needing a boss. So this was accomplished by made up religions and myths to explain the religions as we have read herein to perpetuate the ruling social dis-order of life in those times and still today. We all serve the few and get to eat the crumbs left over from those of us who do the most to perpetuate this ruse.

So piecing together the story of Joseph of Arimathea, Arimathea, being a place that never physically existed as we learned, how did he get this power? Well he got it from his dad.

Joseph's dad put this land of tin empire together by trading with those living in this region and marrying a female Druid who was Jesus' grandmother.

At the time of Jesus, Cornwall was the only known European source of major tin deposits. We can learn more about the Bronze Age when we search the Minoans. The tribes that sailed the seas and went to Lake Superior to mine for tin thousands of years before Jesus. They had the Nefilim maps of the seas and knew the currents that would take them across the Atlantic. Their stories are many. And they deal with the natives from this region and their lives as taught by the Kaloo who taught these few had to live with nature and alchemize it into material.

Scene Nine.   Mary Magdalene and the Other Unseen Ladies on Jesus's Team.

Now who is Mary Magdalene (M) in her real life time?

Mary M was definitely a member of the Core team. From my readings I have learned that she was trained by the Egyptians school of Sacred Knowledge which the Vatican discounted and they called the cult of Isis. For those of narrow mind this was an issue. Isis taught the wonders of nature here on earth as well as the mysteries of the stars and the solar system. Isis in real life was the princess of the Nefilim who was called many names including Inanna. Mary M had her training in this philosophy.

Not everyone involved, now up north in Glastonbury, were from the Essenes school of knowledge, but were part of the wisdoms of all the Sacred Schools the Kaloos created around this olden world of Nefilim urban regions of earth. Those up in this north region were the Druids.

Also Mary M, a woman, caused some concerns in the Hibiru ruling order that have women on the inside not seen as part of the team of the Sadducees or Pharisees. Till this day in the Catholic and organized Jewish tradition so they claim rules, women can not pray with men or be one to lead the prayers except in a subjugated role.

Mary M, I believe as many others do who investigate this event, was to be the keeper of the inner mysteries of this new way. The earth guardian of the highest wisdom. People like Peter, the founder of the so called traditional church could not deal with this truth. Peter tried hard to erase this truth in and around Jerusalem. This was easy to do with Mary M out of the area after the play to show the new way.

In the Gospel of Mary, which can be found I am told in the Nag Hammadi Library translated into English one can read how Mary M told the Disciples what Jesus had told her and the other Apostles secretly. While talking Peter interrupts her and says how do we know Jesus said anything to you at all. Prove it. Jesus was gone and could not be seen in public. So how do you prove the truth? This is the beginning of the physical creation of Christ as opposed to the spirit of love. The eternal love living in the here and now with God of everything in your heart. The kingdom of Heaven right here in your essence.

Jesus the leader did his best to have an even mix of female and male energies to teach and share the new ways. He had his mom Mary. Jesus also had his sister Clare and Martha and Salome. These few have been deliberately removed from the annals of the story except mother Mary who is essential as she had become God's vessel to bring the Messiah with the message of the new way. The new way got so distorted by those who figured out a way to live and feed off Jesus the messenger from the eternal consciousness of all that I call God.

No today's Catholic Church left Jesus on the cross and said he died as a human because of the Jews (Judeans) and because of the Judeans, Jesus now became Christ and we the Catholic Church speak on behalf of Christ. So since they speak for this Roman Empire created god whom they make you believe is the GOD, you must listen to the people they put in charge of the land as their god said these were the real rulers. Later on they put the Pharisees BS in the script by telling you these are god's rules.

But as a Buddhist thought I can hear Paul McCartney, a catholic say, " Mary the mom did come to me as he sings let it be, oh let it be. Singing words of wisdom oh let it be". That's right, shut up and follow the rules. This was what broke up the Beatles. Lennon would not submit to those rules nor would George Harrison. Ringo was the drummer with no reason to shake their tree.

Clare the sister by the way is credited with having quite the Libra personality capabilities of balancing her two sides. She was playful. She shared joy and could be one that could share truths you may not want to hear. She could talk in parables as Jesus did. And share the depths of her wisdom with anyone and everyone.

So now we understand the division of righteousness right from the start. The Christian text based on the Church which Peter is given credit for opening the first Christian Church one was a male domination theme. Father god. The Gnostic sources make it quite clear that Mary M and sister Clare were the balancing source of Mother Nature. Which to this day we still have not learned. We live in and on mother earth's home.

Now let's finish with the spiritual meaning of Jesus and Mary M. Mary M understood the Kingdom of Heaven better than any of Jesus' living Apostles. The Apostles were Core members of setting up the play, living the play and closing the play. The Disciples were important players but were the outer ring. They were not part of the inner circle nor the Core members. The Catholic Church only wants you to know about the Disciples who knew nothing of the play of the Crucifixion.

Mary M was raised in the understanding of the term the Father and the Mother. She knew metaphysical truths. Mary Magdalene lived in both the here and now and the beyond

The real teachings of the inner order of the Essenes taught this Divine energies. The outer communities playing their restricted role of man dominated religious orders did not.

Jesus and Mary M sharing their knowledge together as one must have been fascinating to the few who got it. And so disruptive to the many who see women as a Stepford Wife. A movie of my youth.

When man and woman can combine their energies as one the mysteries of creation will unfold just like a lotus opening up to enjoy the light. Mary M really represents the light of wisdom which the Greeks called Sophie that is lost when we all incarnate here on earth. The true other side that we forget when we serve the masters who run our world. Mary M's energy was the partner Jesus needed to discover with him more and line up together as one with God.

When we plant the seed and wisdom of the goddess Sophie or Isis then the world of the kingdom of heaven will open up again here on earth. We need to eat the apple and awaken from the nightmare we live believing it is the only way.

By the way, the Catholic Church recognizes that Mary M was the teacher of teachers in their own way. Within Roman Catholic traditions Mary M is accorded the title of Apostola Apostolorum. These two Latin words together mean the apostle to the apostles.

Act Ten Epilogue One. Joseph of Arimathea and the Druids

Let's go back to Joseph now living in England. He was living with and under the protection of the ruling order called Druids.

This is another spiritual universe playing out their games In real life. Who are they besides the tribe that Joseph Jr. and his sister Mary, Jesus' Mother, was raised in and went back to when Joseph Senior died and Joseph Jr took over the reigns of his merchant empire.

First off the Celts who lived up in Europe's north west and the Druids came from the same lands. Yes. But they had different beliefs. The Druids like the Essenes were built on an inner and outer circle. Inside was spiritual based. Outside they were beasts who protected their tribes from mankind that was not raised to be civil to begin with.

These tribes escaped the Nefilim rules of order and control. They were the pagans of the woods. They were what Catholic Rome would conquer and control for a period of darkness we call the dark ages.

The outer tribe protected the inner from invasion so the Druids could build their School of Sacred Knowledge. Who gave these tribes that awareness? I believe the Kaloos did. And what the Kaloo were doing is spreading the seeds of awareness. How? By dividing and training different areas to understand a central theme to the message of God is Love and Love is God. You do not worship possessions over life.

The knowledge of the Druids was the natural world of earth. This knowledge was then used to relate to creating a mankind society in tune with nature's.

The Druids wore green. They hid in plain view as a salamander does. The word Druid itself standing alone derives from an oak tree. A "dru" was that word meaning seed of an oak tree. The oak tree was their sacred tree. And oak groves were essential to the Druids ceremonies and practice.

Now it's time for me to introduce a new energy force to us. The Watchers. They like the Kaloos went around educating mankind. These energies were in tune with the stars. They told the Kaloos what this star energy as well as solar energy wanted them to plant as thoughts to grow in mankind's heads.

The Druids complemented the Essenes in a very circular way. If you live the seasons of your thoughts you will escape the issues of duality of life when you believe everything is this and not that way. You need to accept that every thought has its season. To begin, live and grow as well as die. We in living form give thoughts for energy to survive and not just be a passing moment of our existence.

If we can not do that we will kill to continue to live that passing thought. The story of our world today and the imperial religions and imperial governments saying they speak for god, knowing it is not God and not caring about the evil they are about to do to you so you obey.

We have not gone into the Greek schools of sacred learning which began with a sage called Pythagorus. The living man was taught many things by the Watchers with energies and vibrations. The man is given credit for starting universities to teach the creative arts and the sciences of the stars and solar system. These are the vibrations we need to hear so we know what is coming our way.

These schools embraced and thrived on teaching their students the Watchers' world of building a universe. They studied mathematics with an eye for the sacred application associated with numbers, as well as geometry, which became sacred when you learned how to apply it to live in this world of protection afforded you with numbers and the vibration of thoughts those numbers create when put in physical form. Seven is magic because there are three on the bottom and three on top with the fourth vibration the key to life-strive to get even and life will go forward. If not, it becomes a lopsided mess.

The Greek schools taught astronomy as well as cosmology to show and share the energies you are and why you are here. Destiny to achieve your reason to reincarnate or fate to let others use you so they have their destiny at the expense of your living fate.

We are a solid piece of living outer meat but also an inside musical machine tuned to react when we hear a certain note. And I must add this includes being made so we cannot hear the Universe sing to us in this limiting human form. That is until we learn how to communicate with God directly.

The Greek philosophers at their schools put their emphasis on you, the individual's efforts in rising towards the light. Ascending not just reincarnating in an endless cycle of pain and pleasure.

What I never realized till this moment is how many schools existed in Wales and southern England back in the Druids heyday. The students and teachers built communities to learn and ascend that made sure everyone was covered to survive.

Saying all the above there was a gate you must crossover to live this life. At the gate were the protectors of the group who knew they had to kill when they assumed the visitor came to take and not share.

This was a perfect spot to hide Jesus and to share the Gospels of the Crucifixion to end the old way. As well as the Gnostics and open the new way for all to live.

ACT TEN EPILOGUE TWO: The Aftermath and the Order of Melchizedek.

What are the Gnostics in reality? Truths.

Before we leave this section I must bring in the order of thoughts which is called The Order of Melchizedek.

What is this?

How many thoughts of energies are there? Who knows but as we have learned they all physically fall into three categories. One builds communities or administering communities by having a ruler and his ruling crew. To keep you in line they will have a god of some sorts to say this is what I want you to do. Behave as you are being told. Sadducees styled order.

The second line is to have the ruling god of above give you the rules that become your way of life. An order will appear saying this is what god gave us and we must all live in this order. Pharisees styled order.

The third line is a community based on equality led by elders who earned their roles. Not by family or payments but a community where the people become a federation of equals and they live in the here and now and share the present of physical life. They live exploring the opportunities life presents to learn and grow in both the here and now as well as what the future will bring.

This order is hard to define. As today in the history of mankind, we with our mankind controls have yet to create the balance of wants and needs to balance and become the land where we learn to live and share life as individuals and a community of mankind.

The Essenes order tried to plant this seed. The lives they lived are in the Akashic record books that with an open mind you can relive the how and why.

We are a combination of earth's physical needs and energy driven wants from the Stars and the Universal Solar System and the Galaxies plus what has yet to be created. But maybe this Universe that we live in is just a playground to discover what consciousness will do if allowed to have the option of free will. Free will when you begin. And to see how long it takes you to sell your individual physical soul for one's wants and needs which are all an illusion.

And you can hear the creator of all say to you so you thought you can tell Heaven from Hell. Blue skies from pain. A smile through a veil. I just wish you were here with me. Keep trying again you will return.

The game of ascending or reincarnating in this universe that is your prison cell. Everything you wish you had but it was not good enough so you followed some pied piper of thought and became their experiment trying to live in physical bliss which is impossible.

Now to the Order of Melchizedek.

The Essenes had their order with the inner and outer worlds of really a cell's existence. A consciousness cell made to grow and plant a new way to physically live. A way to change the natural order of what then existed and its time has come and gone. By the way, just a thought to share with you that we can delve into later on this is how the CIA, Mossad, KGB, MI6 and the Jesuits as well as Isis, Hezbollah and Al Qaeda operate to name a few with an outer, inner, core trident.

The quarantine of 2020 is the wake up call. The trumpets blaring in my head telling me to sit and finish this Book of Earth series and the spirits that ran rampant here using mankind's consciousness to play their games as to when will the people say enough is enough. Possessions and greed is not the way to have and share physical life.

But the inner order I have discovered was the outer order of the real game. Or at least the game that I am able to perceive at this point in time.

The inner order of the inner order of the Essenes is the Kaloos.

But who is the inner order of the Kaloos?

My friends, it is not the Order Of Melchizedek. The Order as it was labeled in the Old Testament Bible. This Order was the Order that created the Sadduccees and Pharisees. The Essenes and the Kaloos and the Watchers were here to help us overthrow the dark energies that the Order of Melchizedek imposed on this dimension when the isle of Undal sank from this dimension. In Opus 3 the Emerald Tablets of Thoth you will learn what I believe to be true that has locked our consciousness in a living hell. What you are about to read is what the devil's energy that controls our plateau wishes me to believe. The Order of Melchizedek in Act Eleven of this play very cleverly turned the Crucifixion and the Essenes way into a dark energy called Christ the authoritarian god, with his minions called the Vatican and their tributary Christian sects. An absolutely brilliant chess move.

Yes, the Order is actually written in the Bible of our controlling thoughts. The Bible that exposes the origins of mankind hidden in the written words. The old testament tells the stories of the Nefilim and their space travelers for earth called the Anunnaki. This bible again shares the stories of two gods children and families. Their Nefilim born children and their children made from the wombs of their creation mankind shows you the chaos that these races made on earth. It shows you how there was no love, just control. But then it stops when Marduk is dead. Prophets appear saying when the message of who we are and what we are to do will come and share the gospel.

In the absence of these dead gods' rules and order are made to run the world of their urban Anunnaki sites all paying tribute to the return of Marduk with absolute rulers or rules and order paying tribute to Enlil and his rules and order with the guideline notes called Ten Commandments. The Ten Commandments which all the Inner and Core members of the Imperial Religions and Imperial Governments break to keep you under their control. Under their thumb.

If you follow either of these imperial societies you too, according to their rules, can go to heaven and sit with the gods of Nibiru in their everlasting Nibiru physical life.

We were created to be the Anunnaki slaves and servants. They had jobs to do when exploring and Colonizing Earth. The Anunnaki wanted slaves and servants who could do the chores but not live their lives.

Someone put our essence into these bodies. Someone got us to enter the womb of creation. Someone knew how to crack the barrier of eternal existence to physical life. Someone opened this portal. The portal to earth dimension.

We came originally to serve. We were sheep people's consciousness. Then the game changed and we are living in this upheaval of this dimension.

The original monopoly of the Order of Melchizedek control of our consciousness in this dimension called Earth, to serve and be a slave is no longer exclusive. Other energies came into this dimension to sow the seeds of love and fears to play with us to see the limits of what we will take before we wake up and say enough is enough. There is another way i.e.the spear of the Trident to balance the clockwise energies destroying Mother Earth called Imperial Religions and Imperial Governments. The Imperial Religions and Imperial Governments by the dark energies that need to end are themselves run by the Order of Melchizedek.

The Old Testament Bible refers to this order very briefly. Let's look at the translated in English thoughts written in Psalm 110;1,4. The Lord said unto my Lord, sit thou at my right hand. The Lord hath sworn, and will not repent, thou are a priest for ever after the Order of Melchizedek.

Again I must ask who wrote the Bible? Why did they write the Bible? Which version are you reading? Ask yourself and you may see the matrix that controls you.

Many explanations exist by others, who wish to control you in their thought process as to the meaning of these words. I wish to just open you up so you see the Universal picture as opposed to seeing only the latest stroke to keep you numb to Universal truths.

Now my interpretation is different then most as I will include my awareness of the Nefilim who called their rulers Lords with the top Lord on the hierarchy King with his Queen. Here on earth these Lords were also called gods.

What is the meaning of forever? It is not evermore. Forever is only as long as the thought of forever and the world it represents exist. It is not all thoughts.

My Lord is not identified. But if you look to a reference of my Lord in a chapter of Hebrews (New Testament) chapter 6:20 is the following words " whither the forerunner is for us entered, even Jesus (obviously changed as there was no letter "J" at the Jesus's time of life or before, as we learned), made a high priest forever after the Order of Melchizedek".

What is the book of Hebrews? It is in the new testament and is a code/clue to discover the truth of the game Jesus and the Essenes played on the establishment of his time. This game planted the seed that the order of control saying this is what a One God wants you to do is a lie. Their establishment game was to give you two choices which is the game we still live in today. That is the reason for the Essenes game as we have read. There is more than A or B.

In the next chapter of Hebrews Chapter 7 Section Three the Melchizedek, King of Salem (peace) says "without father, without mother, without descent, without having neither beginning of days, nor end of life; but made like unto the son of God; abideth a priest continually.

Ok the words point you to believe Jesus is the son of god. What is god? Is it God? Everything is God. To know God you must see God in all not just you and the object you are receiving for your thought at the moment. We are all God's children. But we live where we must serve the god that we are told owns us. And again we came from a mother called Earth. Where is the mother? Where is LOVE?

If you see the world as I just described taught to us in the Essenes play you see a description of a powerful ascending being. So now if you see this, then you can see that his order belongs to God's Kingdom and all the realms of light. Not just our realm of darkness which shadows the light you are told you are not yet ready to understand. Next time is what religion called Christianity tells you.

The seeds of destruction of A or B are buried in the words of controlled thoughts that limit your ability to perceive the truth. That is why these societies based on secrets are oral and need a teacher, an elder who studies and understands the big picture. Understanding by living life in all its forms.

Remember we live on earth and if we are not trained to open our third eye and use our intuition, with critical thinking, we will only see what our physical kind understands. Our physical mind can only understand the space time continuum that governs earth and its physical dimension. Earth is earth's rules. Not Universal truths. But rules of earth's truths to live in this machine body that earth created for us to live in and experience physical earth life.

Earth, herself, is incapable of preventing the energies from beyond to come to Earth. Mankind is in theory the sons and daughters of Mother Earth that are totally capable of preparing the shield or act as the sword to stop energies from coming into our Earth's atmosphere as well as landing in physical form, such as a meteorite, on Earth. Instead we use our guardianship to create weapons of mass destruction, chemicals to poison our air and water and food that is chemically modified organisms that can not reproduce on their own.

So let's get out of controlled thoughts and go beyond. What is the Order of Melchizedek in spiritual Universe truths?

The Order in Hibiru tradition was actually called the Aleph Etz Melchizedek. The word Aleph is derived from alpha. Alpha is derived from Aleph and means beginning. Truth. What came first, the chicken or the egg? Maybe they both start at the same time.

Etz means tree. And the three words put together mean the beginning of the tree of Melchizedek here on earth. So following this line the tree of mankind's life was planted at that earth time by a great Teacher or maybe a dark teacher within the Melchizedek Universal disorder of thoughts reduced to physical existence.

This is the inner spiritual meaning of mankind's written description of the Order of Melchizedek.

The Order was composed of those who knew how to stop the unseen from being physically seen. They knew how to corral and cross the dimension of time and space and take our collective consciousness and enslave us in dense physical bodies of their creation where light does not naturally come in.

The ad for your consciousness to come to earth was spoken by Rod Serling in his Twilight Zone monologue. The dialog which I will now modify to fit this script. You're traveling through another dimension not only of sight and sound but of physical existence. A journey into a wonderful land whose boundaries are that of imagination. That's the signpost up ahead. Say yes and enter Earth.

You are now an actor in the Order of Melchizedek. The Order has twisted our ability to perceive eternal truths so that they are the living physical guardians of this universe and they shall control you by limiting your ability to freely dream. You are now part of their experiment. Welcome to Earth where your individual incarcerated soul is jailed in our world domination physical order.

So now I must share with you a naked truth. The Order of Melchizedek were the elders of Nibiru or the ones that controlled the elders of Nibiru which we read about in Opus One. Enki was the black sheep of this family of rulers. He did everything he could to get darkness out of our planet. He discovered the love of a Father God as he was the father that locked our consciousness in his altered DNA when he made mankind from the apes. And as the father of mankind he could not just let his creations perish at the time of The Xrossing which our books called the Great Flood as described in Opus 1.

We earthlings had an energy that came to earth from the beyond to change the earth game to try a new order of living here on earth. And that energy were the Essenes central actors playing their roles in the Crucifixion. Lead actor was the running back called SSU as he first introduced himself to me when I was four.

I did not know who this was but I asked my parents and they said do not tell anyone spirits talk to you. This SSU is whom we call Jesus today. And this essence told me one day in my meditation that he was not Christ. "Never said I was and did all I could to NOT have the world believe in the control those running a community used my energy to imprison the minds of so many and those they could not imprison get others to kill". This is not my message.

Remember all universes must have a sun that gives the energy that creates the gravitational force to make a universe work. This universe creates thought or else none of the planets and their living owing moons and asteroids of thought and their wombs that bring into existence physical dense life would ever exist. Jesus was our consciousness' sun's mercury. Jesus came to give us the message of more than forever but also forever more eternal life in all life's various forms.

Now let's go another step further in this spiritual explanation. This coming Messiah, the messenger who came as Jesus in our interpretation is not the Elohenu Melchizedek. This is the diversion and this is how they tried to twist the light of Jesus into the dark energy I call Christ.

The literal translation of Elohenu is the glory of God. But that is black and white. The spiritual meaning is the Divine creative flowering. A flowering of thoughts for us all to smell and believe the scent when we are ready to inhale and hopefully never stop inhaling the thoughts of love.

Now please see that Jesus and his teammates collectively as well as individually were the energy force that seeded this thought of love, unconditional love in our earth controlled minds. And that energy created the metaphysical true shell which we need to fill with love not rules of order and control. Jesus the energy is the antichrist of control.

Jesus came to end the Order of Melchizedek. The letters being OM. OM the vibrations that will set you free from the controlling tree of fear mixed with hate that classifies you so you believe you are what you are told you are. Not one of us.

Here is a thought to share with you. Let's look at the Essenes as really roving ambassadors of spiritual education. These few appear whenever we are stuck in mud of physical existence. As time now exists to help transformation to help the others receive and understand the light they are not perceiving. As light is not in structures, black and white techniques or ideas bounded by schools of written rules and resulting order. The black and white is the Order of Melchizedek. You only can be released from this bond date when you learn to hear the vibrations from the Universe not just the cries of Mother Earth.

To be an elder and become a true capable leader for all, you must have detachment from mammon and all its resulting orders of control to perpetuate the ownership of property over people and our consciousness of oneness. The light helps you see the heart of things. The energy of true existence. See the true existence as the universal light that true existence is, not through the lens of just your physical existence and its illusions of grandeur.

Then, to share the paths of truth with others, you need to have the ability to take the social abuse you will endure as many or really most are programmed to not perceive and not yet ready to become enlightened. My current fate.

Be it Jesus or Buddha the inner truths are hidden in the spoken word that must flower and not be reduced to physical black or white pages. Not the linear A or B but the circle of everything. Now the naked truth is we live under the guise of a father god that rules our living order. We have totally disregarded Mother Earth and the feminine energy of existence as equal to our balance of life.

The sacred story of Mary Magdalene with Jesus is the parable to open our eyes to the end game of understanding we are all at birth both masculine and feminine energy. We are searching for the yin and yang. Life needs a balance.

The role of the Kaloo was to guide the Essenes to establish the communities that would help the light come into physical existence by using the sacred geometry to transport supernatural cosmos energy that was needed to plant this seed of transformation. The seed being the sacred meaning of the

Crucifixion and survival. To understand we do not die. We just move on. The real God of existence does not kill God's children. The nature of earth life does only end your body's physical existence when the energy that moves the hearth and our inside water supply leaves our body.

Learn this. Nature is derived from the Latin word natura. Natura distinguishes man's consciousness from the material of man's body. The concept focuses on the life given and the nurturing aspects of nature by embodying it, in the form of the mother. In essence you get your mother's blood but you are your own consciousness.

Let's go to the word "kaloo". The letters KA when said create a sound which goes back to the sound Mer-Ka-Bah. This sound was once part of a mystic cult way back in our earth time. The triangle of light-spirit-soul.

The Universe is not divided into fun- de- mental realities. The Universe is integrated into the oneness of all thoughts in which none must control the existence of all. Unfortunately today there are the few who believe it is their role to teach their Kabal as black and white rules which are really nothing more than rubble to control your minds. Not the spirit that was taught to open your minds and see how you are controlled. It shares how you are controlled so you can master the game of that control for the benefit of you and you alone.

The Kabal called the Kabbalah is nothing but the perpetuation of trying to understand the Order of Melchizedek getting you to believe that this is all that exists. The mystic interpretation of Enlil's attempt to control mankind to follow the rules of the Animal Farm that the Nefilim created here to rule earth. Learn these rules and you can go to the top of this mind controlled way of existence here on earth.

The Kaloos which I believe were part of Enki's love and resonate to being came to shake up the world of order and control of Enlil the brother and Marduk the son of Enki. They did it by planting the seeds of love. It was the first time in anyone's books on the history of man that love was spoken about was by Jesus. Not Buddha. Not Confucius. Not any of the earlier leaders of religion or philosophical thoughts.

The Greeks went looking for love and searching for that holy grail and falling in line with the Imperial Governments of that time were slaughtered by the Romans who even stole the Greek Gods and gave them Roman names. An example being Zeus, now Jupiter. The Romans came and killed them over who controlled the trading routes of their region. Then they created a game called Christianity using the moral sentiments of Plato searching for understanding as proof that their version of god was naked truth.

So now let me bring us to our conclusion of existence in physical form.

Act Ten The Intended Conclusion to Help One Ascend.

What is light?

Light is everything and everything has light. We need to wake up and take off our shades that prevent you from opening the vortex called your third eye to live and experience eternal life.

We live to ascend. And when we fail we get to do it again in the cycle of reincarnation.

I have been taught in thoughts hard to explain in black and white that there are three stages in the process of rising to the light. Just feel the flow as opposed to seeing black and white as you read this section.

Stage one is becoming aware, a Deep Knowing. Deep knowing is where the forms of life and the boundaries of their physical beings begin to dissolve. You can feel their existence as more than just what you see. All life is from a consciousness. Plants too. Accept and try to understand that truth in a much elevated form. This is really the seed of the story of the Crucifixion of Jesus planted when you understand the spiritual meaning of the game this team Essenes played.

Ever ask yourself what a dolphin or whale means to the energies of our water? Then go to the next step and see how these energies balance the earth in vibrations of sounds. Vibrations that bring in the energies of the stars and solar systems here and there and everywhere else.

These Aquarian life forms are essential to our earth's existence. We are all water created. We are vibrations of consciousness locked into body form. I know it but it is so hard to live that awareness.

I spent my life digging the dirt of shadows and fears to discover the eternal truths more than just the Universe truths. We are all part of an outer reality run by our inner thoughts.

Stage two is Integration. This occurs when we learn to live the level of Deep Knowing every breath we take. Every move we subsequently take. The Integration is now becoming aware of our true nature. We are more than just a body that we use as our vehicle to experience physical life here on earth.

This is a self realization that my spiritual guide and guru Paramhansa Yogananda lived to plant these seeds of thoughts in our western minds. As those in the eastern schools of sacred knowledge were well aware of these truths which they could follow to ascend or use as prison bars for the others to be imprisoned and controlled to continue serving the few who know the truth.

The third stage is Ascension. This is the flowering stage. Where we stop being caterpillars. We become the butterflies that our essence is here to do not the moths who could not ascend because we just could not let go of our small EGO. Small EGO being where we edge the God of everything out to believe in the physical god of our minds limited experience.

Another way to look at this process is to realize it is the process of getting an ego in reverse. Just let it go. Lose your EGO.
This section is what Jesus shared if you spiritually read the vibrations of his thoughts to those who see more as opposed to those who can only hear what the system of control has programmed them to believe and worship.

Jesus took the god of the heavens which controls mankind's olive of life. Jesus helps us squeeze the oil and get to its core and discover that the beauty of life and the eternal joys of existence is God and that God lives inside our energy machine source- the heart. The Crucifixion tried to make you understand that your individual heart is the temple of God. Remember the living stage we are all now in together is temporary. We have the spirit from the beyond of consciousness that this earth gives us this form to learn and ascend.

When you learn to ascend and experience the eternal joys of wholeness and oneness you have entered the Kingdom of everything and have rejoined God in this perfect life without pleasures or pain just awareness that Love unconditionally is the answer to existence and being.

Jesus and his teammates tried to give us a shortcut back to God. Not what the other sages have taught us to do. Just go there and understand God and your wholeness can be right here and right now.

This life not next time. No, right NOW.

Let's ascend. Let's make the third rail of existence govern our community called mankind living here in nature called earth.

Let's build the community of mankind based on love with community support to allow the community to survive and the individual to achieve their dreams of building teams that share the beauties and glory of helping us in physical form become collectively more than we were.

I am a dreamer. My goal is to help us all realize that dreams do come true without selling your soul to accomplish your perceived happiness.

Now let's move on to Act Eleven. The Creation of Manmade Christ.

Calvary Hill

Glastonbury Landmark

Herod Coins

Holy Roman Empire Logo

Order of Melchizedek

Sitting in Jaffa.

Temple in Nazareth where it is said Jesus sopke.

The Sea of Galilee Where I sat and caught this feather from heaven.

Jesus's footprint, it is said.

www.ingramcontent.com/pod-product-compliance
Lightning Source LLC
LaVergne TN
LVHW011737060526
838200LV00051B/3209